PLANT

IN A
TINY SPACE

31-Daily Devotions

MELANIE PADILLA

WESTBOW
PRESS®
A DIVISION OF THOMAS NELSON
& ZONDERVAN

WestBow Press books may be ordered through booksellers or by contacting:

WestBow Press
A Division of Thomas Nelson & Zondervan
1663 Liberty Drive
Bloomington, IN 47403
www.westbowpress.com
844-714-3454

Because of the dynamic nature of the Internet, any web addresses or links contained in this book may have changed since publication and may no longer be valid. The views expressed in this work are solely those of the author and do not necessarily reflect the views of the publisher, and the publisher hereby disclaims any responsibility for them.

Any people depicted in stock imagery provided by Getty Images are models, and such images are being used for illustrative purposes only. Certain stock imagery © Getty Images.

Scripture quotations marked TPT are from The Passion Translation®. Copyright © 2017, 2018, 2020 by Passion & Fire Ministries, Inc. Used by permission. All rights reserved. ThePassionTranslation.com.

Scripture quotations marked (NIV) are taken from the Holy Bible, NEW INTERNATIONAL VERSION®, NIV® Copyright © 1973, 1978, 1984, 2011 by Biblica, Inc.® Used by permission. All rights reserved worldwide.

Scripture quotations marked (KJV) are taken from the King James Version, public domain.

Scripture quotations marked AMPC are taken from the Amplified Bible Classic Edition (AMPC) , Copyright © 2015 by The Lockman Foundation, La Habra, CA 90631. All rights reserved.

Scripture quotations marked (AMP) are taken from the Amplified Bible, Copyright © 1954, 1958, 1962, 1964, 1965, 1987 by The Lockman Foundation. Used by permission.

All Scripture marked with the designation "GW" is taken from GOD'S WORD®. © 1995, 2003, 2013, 2014, 2019, 2020 by God's Word to the Nations Mission Society. Used by permission.

Scripture quotations marked (MSG) are taken from THE MESSAGE, copyright © 1993, 2002, 2018 by Eugene H. Peterson. Used by permission of NavPress. All rights reserved. Represented by Tyndale House Publishers, Inc.

ISBN: 979-8-3850-3743-8 (sc)
ISBN: 979-8-3850-3744-5 (e)

Library of Congress Control Number: 2024923304

Print information available on the last page.

WestBow Press rev. date: 11/26/2024

CONTENTS

ACKNOWLEDGMENTS

To my son, I love you, and God bless you.

To all my family and church family members, I love you, and God bless you.

I want to give a special thanks to my friend Roxanna for motivating me to get this book done.

To all the families and single people without a home, I pray that the good Lord Jesus provides swiftly for you. I encourage you to continue to pray, believe, and not give up, in Jesus' name.

And to all who read this book, I pray and believe that these words will encourage you and that the Lord Jesus may bless you all, in the mighty name of the Lord Jesus Christ, amen and amen.

PLANT IN A TINY SPACE

Look at this plant.
This flower looks just like the sun.
Cradle and protect
From the Most High is done.
Every second, every minute,
Fruit begins to enliven.
The roots remain young.
And even after all that has happened,
So it still grows.
There was a time
When its shine
Thereupon devoured
With all her petals missin,'
And the sun rarely glistened.
High wind gusts,
Waiting for a shower of rain.
But around a time in May,
He who is up on high sees her face
And gives her a token of remembrance
Of the beauty she still contains.
He steadily rebuilds her.
She stands in awe at each new miracle!
She always thanks God for
Each new way to prosper.

Day 1

CHILD OF THE MOST HIGH

———⁓⁓⊙⊙⊙⊙⊙⁓⁓———

*Like newborn babies, crave pure spiritual milk, so that by it you may grow
up in your salvation. Now that you have tasted the Lord is good.*
—1 PETER 2:2 (NIV)

"Knock, knock, knock." It was a police officer at the door.

"Yes, officer, how can I help you?"

"We have been told by DCFS to come and pick up a fifteen-year-old Melanie Padilla."

"Sir, you cannot legally take this child. You need an order from the court."

After some time debating back and forth, the officers finally left us alone and drove off. I was sixteen years old, it was summertime, and my father had passed away on the previous before. He'd had a brain aneurysm in church while giving a testimony to the youth, which he had titled, "Don't Do Drugs, Please."

I felt the love of God even in those most horrible times. I checked myself into a Christian women's home in La Puente, California, the day after my dad went to be with the Lord. It was there that I first experienced the greatness of the Lord and truly felt the genuine love from God through his people. I recall this part of my life, and I remember how I felt as a child—innocent, hurting, but still able to feel the love of God. I wasn't worried or feeling down in my spirit.

The Bible says to crave pure spiritual milk like a child does. That way, we can grow up in him.

PRAYER

Lord, my God, thank you for loving me so much. Help me to be aware of your loving presence every day of my life. Amen.

Day 2

HOLY SPIRIT, COME QUICKLY!

———•••———

Hasten, O God, to save me; come quickly, LORD, to help me.
—PSALM 70:1 (NIV, EMPHASIS ADDED)

One hot Friday, I was extremely motivated to get my license, so I went to the Department of Motor Vehicles in Los Angeles. When my number was called, I approached the worker, only to be confronted with bad news. My license had been suspended, and I had to go to court to get it fixed. I had to walk home, so I had basically come all the way there for nothing. Since things did not work out the way that I wanted them to, I wanted to suppress the negative feelings by going to the store and purchasing a cigarette so that I could smoke. Suddenly, it came to my mind—a remembrance of a sermon that a pastor had said one beautiful Sunday: "There's a prayer that we can pray, and that's to ask the Holy Spirit to act quickly. Let's challenge ourselves to do that when we're tempted to sin."

So I went to the restroom, and I said, "Holy Spirit, come quickly because I am about to sin." I was following what the pastor said to do during circumstances like this one. I began to walk toward the liquor store. Right before I got there, this very large car pulled up in front of me and blocked my way. A person inside asked me if I needed a ride home. I peered inside closely to see who the people were. I recognized the family as members of a church I was going to every Sunday. God answered my prayer. Wow!

PRAYER

Father, my God, Lord, and Savior, thank you for listening to all the words that I say to you. Help me say, "Holy Spirit, come quickly," before I sin when I get upset.

Day 3

RELIEF FROM GRIEF

—————•••————

You did it: you changed wild lament into whirling dance; you ripped off my black mourning band and decked me with wildflowers. I'm about to burst with song; I can't keep quiet about you. GOD, my God, I can't thank you enough.
—PSALM 30:11 (MSG)

"We don't think your dad is going to make it." I had just received a call, and it was 2:00 a.m. I had received really bad news. My father had been in church giving a testimony when he suddenly experienced what the doctors called a brain aneurysm.

I cried and cried and cried. Then I became angry and went to talk to the pastor after the funeral. I wanted to tell him how upset I was with God. Just before I opened my mouth, he interrupted me with these words: "You know that the body is just a shell. *Mija*, your dad is a man of God." And immediately, the peace of God that surpasses all understanding fell upon me. I knew I was going to see my dad again.

I thank the Lord because at times like this, he confirms his Word in our lives. It is so beautiful when the joy of the Lord is poured into our hurting hearts.

PRAYER
....
God, my God, your love is everlasting and purposefully distributed to me daily. You are always reminding me of how much you love me.

Day 4

CORRUPTED THINKING

Therefore, my heart is glad, and my tongue rejoices; my flesh also dwells secure.
—PSALM 16:9 (NIV)

I was in the library one day when I noticed an old email of mine popping up in my library account's web page. I was tempted to become frightened for many odd reasons. I thanked the Lord Jesus that his mighty and Holy Spirit constantly reminded my soul that I was now a *new creation in Christ.* The brutal pattern of corrupted thinking was slowly being changed by the power of God (Father, Son, and the Holy Spirit).

The times that I have tried to accomplish this on my own haven't worked or stayed. I have received great news, which is now, I am dependent on God, and I am perfectly fine with being so. He has already won the victory, and therefore, he has the transformation power that I need and gladly wish to receive. Being followers of Christ and having received the Holy Spirit mean that he dwells inside us, so we have victory already living within us. Isn't that amazing? And it's true too. So take your eyes off what the enemy is doing and focus on what God is doing.

PRAYER

Lord, my heavenly Father, thank you for the gift of Jesus. I am truly glad that I may experience true eternal life here on earth just like the Bible tells us about. Help me to keep my eyes on what you're doing instead of what the devil is doing. Amen.

Day 5

ACCEPTED WHEN REJECTED

———∿∽◦◦◦◦◦∿———

Come to him [the risen Lord] as to a living Stone which men rejected and
threw away, but which is choice and precious in the sight of God.
—1 PETER 2:4 (AMP)

"I'm sorry, but we want you to leave our home." I was thrown out of a family member's house as a teenager. They were afraid for the safety of their children because of me being there. I had been diagnosed with the human immunodeficiency virus. To be honest, I was only fourteen years old at the time, and it was just a month or so after a doctor had told me this diagnosis. I was not upset with my family for throwing me out because of this. I completely understood their point of view. They were probably just nervous and protective of their two little children, which included a newborn child. I knew Jesus still loved me even though I did not completely understand the situation. What I did understand, though, was that Ephesians 3:19 said that God's love surpassed human understanding.

I know God constantly shows the unconditional nature of his love and reminds us that no matter what the world thinks of us, we are *still* valuable. Let me remind you that you are a very fine treasure in the eyes of God.

PRAYER

Thank you, Lord. You're an amazing God. My God, you're so awesome. My Father loves me beyond words. His love is even more than unconditional. It is far beyond human understanding. Thank you.

Day 6

BLESS WITH YOUR WORDS

—⁓∿⌒⌒⌒⌒⌒⌒∿—

When I was a child, I talked like a child, I thought like a child, I reasoned like a child; now
that I have become a man, I am done with childish ways and have put them aside.
—1 CORINTHIANS 13:11 (NIV)

"I have a drug problem." I was just beginning high school, and I had met a guy on the party line. Very quickly after meeting this man, I was in a romantic relationship with him. Adults in my life already knew my pattern of going to school, coming home, and so on. They noticed a shift and questioned where I was spending my time. Also, the only friend I usually hung out with was the neighbor next door. When they went to look for me there, I was nowhere to be found. So it was easy for them to see a change in my normal routine. They began to ask, "Do you have a drug problem?" or "What is it?"

I said, "Yes, I do have a drug problem."

They asked me, "What kind of drug?"

I had to come up with an answer quickly, so I told a lie. "It's meth." I lied about having a drug problem. I was sent to this youth drug program where they held classes once a week. As long as I was attending those classes one to two times per week, I was fine—*fine* because nobody was asking about my whereabouts. I did not get to finish those classes because I was introduced to meth and became addicted during the process.

James 3:10 in the Amplified Bible says, "Out of the same mouth come *both* blessing and cursing. These things, my brothers, should not be this way [for we have a moral obligation to speak in a manner that reflects our fear of God and profound respect for His precepts]." This is an example of my own experience, which led me to believe that we should be careful to use our words and to choose to say positive instead of negative things or lies.

PRAYER

Lord, my God, please help me to become more encouraging, caring, kind, and loving through my words. If I ever get off track and use negativity through my words, please remind me that I am representing you and kindly guide me back to the way of everlasting truth. Thank you also for always forgiving me. Amen.

Day 7

WEB OF DECEIT

———$\sim$o·e·$\mathcal{S}$·o·$\mathcal{S}$·o·o·w———

Thus says the Lord of hosts: Do not listen to the words of the [false] prophets who prophesy to you. They teach you vanity (emptiness, falsity, and futility) and fill you with vain hopes; they speak a vision of their own minds and not from the mouth of the Lord.
—JEREMIAH 23:16 (AMPC)

During the holidays in a group home, I was always feeling extra sad, not only because of having to spend Christmas and Thanksgiving with strangers in a group home but mainly because I wanted to go to church, and I was not allowed to. I was referred to the chaplain, who was the "best" that the people in charge could do. The chaplain was described as "remarkably awesome." I was entirely convinced that I should visit with "her" because it would be beneficial.

One day I was feeling sad, so I went to go see the chaplain. And oh my, I felt worst after having that visit with her. Why? I wasn't sure at the time, but I knew it was something internal going on that was disturbing me. I see now that I was experiencing disappointment and sadness in my heart because the chaplain was a "he-she." The chaplain was a senior lady who was dressed like a guy. (My intentions are not to offend anyone, but I am only sharing my experience as a child in a group home for girls.)

This was not what I was taught as a child in a Christian church. But in my true story when I was sixteen years old, I was told it was OK. As young as I was, I already knew and felt in my heart that it was not OK. The proof to that was the part that I explained: I felt worse after I left my visit with the chaplain.

The prayer on this page is going to be personal. You can read and agree if you choose, which you should. Jesus loves all of you.

PRAYER
....

Thank you, Father God, who is heaven. Praise your wonderful name. I love you, and I know you love us all. I just want to lift these young teenage girls up in prayer. I pray that they do not lose hope in you. Show them in their everyday lives that you love and care for them regardless of the circumstances around them, in Jesus's name, amen and amen.

Day 8

LET YOUR WORDS BE FEW

Do not be hasty with your mouth, speaking careless words or impulsive in thought to bring up a matter before God. For God is in heaven and you are on earth; therefore, let your words be few.
—ECCLESIASTES 5:5 (AMP)

Jesus loves you and me both. He cares about us, and there is no doubt about that. He is sovereign, and he is capable of answering each of our prayers. This is what the Bible calls being hasty. The Lord hears our prayers, and he is sovereign and high above the clouds, even higher than all the planets. He sees us and knows when we are affected by our circumstances. He even knows when we are affected by other people's circumstances. God especially knows what we feel—happy, sad, mad, angry, nervous, worried, and even desperate.

At some point in my life, I had made a promise to God (with spoken words) because I wasn't sure if he cared enough to answer my prayer. I also did not feel it was important enough. Imagine a dad who knows that his child is going through a tough time. The dad can evidently presume this because of his child's excessive crying or change in behavior and attitude. So *because* the dad is concerned, he tells his child, "Please come talk to me." This is the same with our God. When we talk to him, it is because we trust him to hear our words. We believe that he really does care when we talk to him. You are important.

PRAYER

Lord, my God, help me to confide in you. I want to have confidence to speak about what burdens me. I know you hear my words. It would be nice for me to demonstrate that I am trusting in the Lord just like the Bible tells me to.

Day 9

STATE OF THE ART

—⁓⁓⚬⚬⚬⚬⚬⚬⚬⚬⁓⁓—

I can anticipate the response that is coming: "I know that all God's commands are spiritual,
but I'm not. Isn't this also your experience?" Yes. I'm full of myself after all, I've spent a long
time in sin's prison. What I don't understand about myself is that I decide one way, but then
I act another, doing things I absolutely despise. So, if I can't be trusted to figure out what
is best for myself and then do it, it becomes obvious that God's command is necessary.
—ROMANS 7:14–16 (MSG)

"Lady, you're not going anywhere, so what are you talking about?"
"No, ma'am, what are you talking about? I must leave. I have things to take care of."
I was in the hospital, and I had just come out of surgery. I forgot that I could not feel my legs. While I was lying in a hospital bed, I urged the nurses to disconnect me from all the machines and take me outside in a wheelchair so that I could catch a taxi home. I should have stayed in the hospital for the period of time that I had been advised to, but I did not do that. I actually left to take care of some things. The condition that I was in did not get better; it got worse.

Maybe you have made this mistake or have seen somebody else make this mistake. I call it a life lesson rather than a mistake because we learn and get better at responding to circumstances with the help of the Holy Spirit. God's commands are necessary. They include his holy words, which were spoken in the Bible. He reminds us to take good care of our bodies because he loves us. God wants us to be healthy and to flourish physically. He reminds us of that in the Bible, such as in 3 John 1:2.

PRAYER
....

Lord, my God, thank you for all the promises and reassurances that you are a loving God and that you love me. Please help me to take care of my physical health and not to put postpone it.

Day 10

OUT OF THE MUDDY MUD

——⁓⁓⁓⁓○⁓○⁓○⁓⁓⁓——

At one time we too were foolish, disobedient, deceived and enslaved by all kinds of passions and pleasures. We lived in malice and envy, being hated and hating one another.
—TITUS 3:3 (NIV)

I got high because I did not care anymore. I went home from the hospital to face an eviction notice on my door. A few days later, I was thrown out onto the street, and I became homeless. At that point, I felt lonely and hopeless. I turned to drugs because I felt like nobody cared, so I did not care either. I know that it does not make sense, but that's the lie I told myself and what I believed. I took actions that corresponded to what I told myself and believed it to be.

I was at a low place at this time. I saw other people around me also living on the streets. I decided to copy what they did to survive. I thought, *Wow! I never imagined it would come to this,* but it did. I became comfortable with being homeless, and I did not see anything wrong in what I was doing. There may have been a family member or a friend or two who were hurt when they saw the spot where I lay, but at the time, I did not care. I was greatly discouraged at two big mountains (problems). First, I was severely ill, and second, I was literally homeless, so how was I going to get better. I saw no hope of getting well again.

Then, I thought a lot about why I was there in the first place. Now, I think a lot about whom? Jesus! He took me out of that dirty place. Jesus saved me from death and took me out of that hopeless state I was in—living homeless on the streets (in a tent), being physically and mentally ill, feeling isolated. I just felt worthless, but Jesus gave me hope. Now, I am not saying that I have it all together, but I know that I am not where I used to be. That's because of the love of God. I hope you read the poem in the beginning of the book. God can save anyone, anywhere.

PRAYER

Jesus, you do not deceive us. You are mighty to save. I want to say thank and glorify you for your mighty works. I know that you love me.

MELANIE PADILLA

Day 11

JESUS LOVES YOU

Is there any place I can go to avoid your Spirit? To be out of your sight? If I climb to the sky, you're there! If I go underground, you're there! If I flew on morning's wings to the far western horizon, you'd find me in a minute—you're already there waiting!
—PSALM 139:7–10 (MSG)

Everywhere you go—everywhere—he is with you. I want to say that whether I was in my own apartment, a hospital bed, a family member's home, or a tent on the sidewalk, Jesus always was, is, and is going to be there. I had tried to hide from him, but he loved me so much that he followed me. He tells us in the Holy Bible—and he cannot lie—that he is the way, the truth, and the life.

I went from sleeping outside of a church to sleeping out on a crate on top of a dirt pile. The sun woke me up every morning, and I took the crate to the other side where there was shade. Soon, the sun followed me to that side and caused my face to burn up once again. Jesus was present in the dark times that I went through, whether it was sunlight waking me up in the morning or a simple smile while I was feeling sad. Another time, I did not have to steal food because somebody gave me a sandwich. Another time, someone gave me a blanket when I was cold.

I love to hear somebody tell me, "Jesus loves you." It can make any day better.

PRAYER

Lord, thank you. I know I can tell myself, *Jesus loves me*, and I will feel better because it is the truth. If I see someone who looks sad, help me to say, "Jesus loves you," because it will also lighten their day.

Day 12

HARMONY AND PEACE

———∿∽◦⟨◦⟨◦⟩◦⟩◦∿———

Then [with a deep longing] you will seek Me and require Me [as a vital necessity]
and [you will] find Me when you search for Me with all your heart.
—JEREMIAH 29:12 (AMP)

While living on the street homeless, a lot of bad things came along with that hopeless lifestyle. I had promiscuous relations. When I had money to buy food, I bought drugs instead. I had a dog while I was on the street, but I then idolized the dog. I was sucked into the small world of addiction, fornication (sex before marriage), poverty, idolatry, lying, stealing, manipulation, sin, sin, and more sin.

But guess what? Because of what Jesus Christ did on the cross, I had the opportunity to become reconciled to him. I just recently read an article by Amanda W. on Christianwebsite.com that defines *reconciliation* in the Bible to bring harmony between God and humans. God hates sin because sin separates us from him. It gets in the way of our relationship with God. Transformation begins with the realization that even though you really messed up, God forgives you for all of it. What should follow that is the removal of those very obstacles that destroy our closeness to God. Colossians 1:21–22 says, "And you, who were alienated and hostile in mind, doing evil deeds, he has now reconciled in his body of flesh by his death, to present you holy and blameless and above reproach before him."

PRAYER

Thank you, Lord Jesus. Let me begin all my prayers with thank you, Jesus. My soul is well with this. I just want to thank you for wiping off the slime from the pit and making me clean as can be.

Day 13

PRIVILEGED CHILDREN

———~~∘∘Ⓔ⦵∘Ⓔ∘∘~~———

It is because of the Lord's mercy and loving-kindness that we are not
consumed, because His [tender] compassions fail not.
—LAMENTATIONS 3:22–23 (KJV)

Gratefully, I am no longer embarrassed to share this story. It was by God's grace that I was blessed with a beautiful one-bedroom apartment, which was even better than the first one I had. This one was furnished and brand new. I had just come from living in a tent and skipping from motel room to motel room to having my own wonderfully furnished apartment. The other great thing about it was that it cost ten dollars to rent.

Two months passed, and I had already started hitting the pipe and hanging with the wrong crowd. About one year after getting the keys to my new place, I was fighting an eviction in court—*again*. Of course, the Lord Jesus Christ walked me through it, and thankfully, I retained my place even though I did not deserve it.

Jesus is so great, y'all, even when you severely mess up and even critically like I did. I was being blessed and was irresponsible at the same time. When the Lord blesses you, he does not do a half job; he goes all the way above and beyond. Unfortunately, sometimes we may not handle his blessing too well. But the positive outcome of it is that we can repent and turn, and the Lord will restore us. Jesus showed himself to be forgiving, loving, and a light in the darkness, just like the Holy Bible says.

PRAYER

Father God, thank you that your Word says you remember my sins no more. Thank you that I have the opportunity to let your light make me shine in any circumstance I am facing. I have joy, joy, joy, joy down in my heart.

Day 14

ENCOURAGE YOURSELF

—wwwwcacacaracacom—

I'm not saying that I have this all together, that I have it made. But I am well on my way, reaching out for Christ, who has so wondrously reached out for me. Friends, don't get me wrong: By no means do I count myself an expert in all of this, but I've got my eye on the goal, where God is beckoning us onward—to Jesus. I'm off and running, and I'm not turning back.
—PHILIPPIANS 3:13-14 (MSG)

You've gotten this far already. Keep pressing toward the goal. In other words, keep on pushing toward being formed into the image of Jesus Christ. You may not be exactly where you want to be. However, give yourself a pat on the back and say thank you Jesus because you know that if you are following Jesus, you are well headed in a meaningful direction. Our lives are meaningful to the Lord Jesus Christ.

It could have begun ten years ago, two years ago, a month ago, or even yesterday. But the point is that you are not how you were back then. You are changing for the better. When you trip up or fall, just repent and turn. He is ready to forgive you after you confess with your mouth (see 1 John 1:9). Change can be anything from changing your diet, to going to the gym, to no longer using curse words, etc. The joy of the Lord is your strength (see Nehemiah 8:10). Ask for the wonderful Holy Spirit to help you become more productive and accomplish more in less time. We can do this with the help of God and can be in a good, refreshing state (untroubled) while doing it.

PRAYER

Thank you, Lord Jesus, for this and every day. Thank you for the trees, the beautiful clouds, and birds that fly above the sky. As I look up into the sky today, let me take a longer look at your beauty.

Day 15

SPEAK LIFE

—ⁿⁿ⁓⁓⁓⁓⁓⁓⁓⁓—

Blessed [fortunate, prosperous, favored by God] is he whose
transgression is forgiven, and whose sin is covered.
—PSALM 32:1-3 (AMP)

"I just want to say I am sorry if I hurt you." It thought very long about whether I should do it or not. It took a guilt trip of about thirty minutes to bring to text these simple words. I remember that it was a day in August when I did not really feel exhilarated about taking the initiative to tells a friend that I was sorry. I did not want to apologize and admit my wrong in a quarrel. Why? Because of one word: *pride.*

Do you know what keeps you from apologizing? It's pride. It is difficult to say to someone who hurt you, "I just want to say thank you, and I am sorry if I hurt you." It's difficult because we don't feel comfortable about coming to an apology. I say many times, "Surely not, Lord," but he nags me to do it until I finally just do it. When I do, it feels so much better. I experience the benefits of forgiveness.

We should pray and believe that we will continue to be open to the benefits of forgiveness. First John 3:18 (ESV) says, "My little children, let us not love in word, neither in tongue; but in deed and in truth." King James version: Proverbs 15:1 says, "A soft answer turneth away wrath: but grievous words stir up anger."

PRAYER

Lord, help me to be a person who speaks life even if it means I should apologize when I do not feel like doing it.

Day 16

AVAILABLE TO BLESSINGS

—⁓⊶⊙⊙⊙⊶⊙⊶⁓—

And all these blessings shall come on thee, and overtake thee, if thou
shalt hearken unto the voice of the LORD thy God.
—DEUTERONOMY 28:2 (KJV)

The boy that I liked sent me a goodbye message. One day when I got home from school, I received some bad news via a DM on Myspace: "I met this girl, and I really like her, so I have to say goodbye to you." Afterward, my chest hurt, and I started crying, which turned to anger. I remembered when my friend Elizabeth had broken up with a guy on Myspace, gone to the bathroom, grabbed a razor blade, and put cuts on her back. I did not understand what she was doing it for. I did not like seeing her do it. Unfortunately, in this situation, I chose to pretend I was like Elizabeth. I chose to deal with the situation the same way that she did it. I went downstairs into the kitchen, took a knife to my room, and tried to do what I saw Elizabeth do. I nearly got the knife to my skin, then just dropped it, and began to cry out to God.

Whoever is born again with Holy Spirit is considered a new creation. Each of us has the ability to hear God's voice and to obey it. When it says, "All these blessings shall come on thee, and overtake thee, it is talking about how these blessings are in storage for you and are guaranteed to come forth as a result of obedient behavior. After feeling the opposition from God with the decision that I was about to make, I quickly listened to him and dropped the knife. I then felt peace and joy from God. I believe that I even had a good dinner and watched a movie after that.

PRAYER

Yes, Father God, thank you for your grace, love, and mercy. Thank you for choosing, creating, and specifically calling me toward your loving presence and into your loving arms. Thank you for embracing me and gently making my day turn into a great one.

MELANIE PADILLA

Day 17

GOD'S GOT YOUR BACK

—————※∾⌒⌒⌒⌒⌒∾※—————

Has anyone by fussing before the mirror ever gotten taller by so much as an inch?
If fussing can't even do that, why fuss at all? Walk into the fields and look at the
wildflowers. They don't fuss with their appearance—but have you ever seen color and
design quite like it? The ten best-dressed men and women in the country look shabby
alongside them. If God gives such attention to the wildflowers, most of them never even
seen, don't you think he'll attend to you, take pride in you, do his best for you?
—LUKE 12:24–28 (MSG)

Do not stress; God has your back. Many times, God's Word reminds us that we do not need to worry about the basic necessities of life. There were a few of these times in my life, but I'll tell you about one in particular. I was worried about having the perfect sweater to wear. I wanted a nice, cute one. I wanted one that went with every outfit I had. I searched everywhere, but I could not seem to find one. I kept searching from store to store until eventually, I just told Jesus, *If you want to bless me by finding one, go ahead. I am giving this thing too much of my attention, and I apologize for that.* About seven days later, I walked into a store to apply for a job, and *boom*, the perfect sweater instantly caught my eye. It was on sale.

I used to take really long when shopping in stores and deciding which items I wanted, when I did not actually need them to begin with. Being content with the things that I already had was the key. Trying to impress other people became a very tiring job. But if I do find myself searching in one aisle of the store too long, I have learned to snap out of it and to ask God for assistance in choosing the correct thing.

PRAYER

Thank you, Lord, for being my provider, redeemer, and supplier. Your wonderful hand sustains me. I ask that impressing you would be my main intent in all that I do throughout the day—even simple things like shopping. Amen.

Day 18

THE KINGDOM OF GOD IS ALREADY IN YOU

Besides, God will give you his constantly overflowing kindness. Then, when you always have everything, you need, you can do more and more good things.
—2 CORINTHIANS 9:8 (GW)

I wonder if I have enough money to buy that. Have you ever bought something that you did not even end up using? The next day, did you find that you were not interested in it anymore? That has happened to me too many times. King James Version: Philippians 4:19 says, "But my God shall supply all your need according to his riches in glory by Christ Jesus." It says in God's Word that he provides for all of our needs. Because I am reminded of this, it means that I should not continue spending foolishly.

My Lord Jesus is loving and gentle, but he also can become angry when we act in self-centeredness. When I go astray, I want Jesus to gently bring me back on the path with him, where I am in harmony with his will. I do not want him to correct me in anger. He is loving, gentle, forgiving and much more. I have to remind myself that I have everything that I need already. New International Version: Luke 17:21 says, "People will not say, 'Look, God's kingdom is here!' or 'There it is!' because the kingdom of God is in your midst."

PRAYER

Lord, thank you. Please help me not to walk with a bag of money that has holes in it. I know that when I go to the store, there are things that I like to buy. But I know that peace, contentment, that I am wonderfully made by you, and what you think of me are most important.

Day 19

TURN YOUR FROWN UPSIDE DOWN!

—~~~∽⟜⟨⟩⟜∽~~~—

You who sit down in the High God's presence, spend the night in Shaddai's shadow,
say this: "God, you're my refuge. I trust in you and I'm safe!" That's right—
he rescues you from hidden traps, shields you from deadly hazards.
—PSALM 91:1 (MSG)

I was very polite, and they acted very mean. One hot day, I applied for a membership at some local gym, and I got instantly denied. I went in there with a positive attitude and got a mean attitude toward me in return. I then went to treat myself to breakfast, and I got treated differently because I ordered from the value menu. I went home and just cried. I cried and told God how I felt. I was hurt that everywhere I went that day, I got the same treatment from everybody, even when I went in there with good intentions and even when I was very kind to every person I encountered. In return, I left feeling execrable. When I cried out to God, my tears turned into ones of happiness because I knew that he was right there with me.

Jesus is real, and he really loves you. Do not get offended. Sometimes you're polite and kind, and people are mean. But you can go somewhere private, cry, tell God how you feel, and then say, "You are my refuge and my God in whom I trust" (see Psalm 91:2). I guarantee that you will feel better.

PRAYER

Lord, you are my God. Jesus, I thank you for your comfort when other people cause me to feel uncomfortable. Thank you that I can privately go into the next room and cry to you. When I say Jesus help me, you hear me, and I feel better.

Day 20

THIS LITTLE LIGHT OF MINE

Here's another way to put it: You're here to be light, bringing out the God-colors in the world. God is not a secret to be kept. We're going public with this, as public as a city on a hill. If I make you light-bearers, you don't think I'm going to hide you under a bucket, do you? I'm putting you on a light stand. Now that I've put you there on a hilltop, on a light stand—shine! Keep open house; be generous with your lives. By opening up to others, you'll prompt people to open up with God, this generous Father in heaven.
—MATTHEW 5:14–16 (MSG)

I felt that reading my Bible in public was the wrong thing to do. Sometimes I felt a little opposition and scared of what might people think of me if I pulled out my Bible in front of them. In fact, it was true because sometimes, people gave me a certain look or moved away from me when I did open my Bible. Sometimes, I wanted to get on my knees and to thank Jesus but then changed my mind because of where I was at or the strangers who might see me.

I've been practicing by writing those thoughts down and pulling out my Bible to read any place and anytime. After all, we are called to be light bearers, so let your light shine.

PRAYER

Lord God, thank you for the Holy Bible. Thank you that true liberty and freedom come from you. You are an original and outstanding God, who fights with and stands right alongside me throughout the day. Any opposing forces in other people around me will be repelled by your anointing, God. I will also treat everyone with kindness and love, regardless of how I get treated in return.

MELANIE PADILLA

Day 21

YOU ARE VALUABLE

———— ∿∿∿∿∿∿∿ ————

But you, Israel, are my servant. You're Jacob, my first choice, descendants of my good friend Abraham. I pulled you in from all over the world, called you in from every dark corner of the earth, telling you, "You're my servant, serving on my side. I've picked you. I haven't dropped you." Don't panic. I'm with you. There's no need to fear for I'm your God. I'll give you strength. I'll help you. I'll hold you steady, keep a firm grip on you.
—ISAIAH 41:10 (MSG)

Jehovah Jireh, Christ Jesus, and the Holy Spirit are one God. It's a wonderful experience to see the manifestation of GOD in our lives and the illumination of the Holy Spirit throughout our lives, throughout our days, and throughout our nights. It is great when this is not just an experience but a big part of our everyday living. I mean, for example, you can look back at prior years of your life and see when you made mistake after mistake, over and over again. You didn't completely fall or die. Jesus saved you and slowly started building you up. You discover that those are his thumbprints.

Now, we can expect to see his whole handprint and footprints very soon! Yeah, we make mistakes, but we get better and better at this with the help of God. We can find the true, comforting assurance that Jehovah Shalom is mighty—almighty! We have his peace, and Jesus is with us the whole way. We can find great comfort in knowing that he is in charge. We can confront this life boldly, gently, and with the power that is in him. We can also have peace in doing this.

PRAYER

Thank you, Jesus, that all the days of my life are valuable to you. You love me, cherish me, and want me to be at peace and in good health and to seek peace in every situation. Help me live in harmony with the people around me. Amen.

Day 22

LOVE AND LIGHT

———⌇⌇⌇⟋⟋⟋⟋⌇⌇⌇⟋⟋———

And walk continually in Love [that is, value one another—practice empathy and compassion, unselfishly seeking the best for others] just as Christ also Loved you and gave himself up for us, an offering and sacrifice to God [slain for you, so that it became] a sweet fragrance.
—EPHESIANS 5:2 (AMP)

CALM

I love the hospital, where you're catered to. I love feeling like someone cares. You can press the button, and a nurse comes in. But there's no better love than what Jesus gives, and he cares much more. He laid down his life for you, and it was a very pleasant aroma. There are blessings in store for you, which he wants to pour down on you. He is more than happy to do so. The first thing that comes to my mind is this: Have you ever been asleep when you smelled somebody cooking breakfast? You roll over, and next thing you know, somebody fixed you a pretty plate—a big plate—with all the favorite things that you enjoy for breakfast. Multiple times, I can remember experiencing this when I was in a hospital bed.

I have even greater times when this happens at church every Sunday. And every time, I feel the illumination of the Holy Spirit. Just say, "Holy Spirit, breathe into me," take in a deep breath through your nose, and ask Jesus to help you experience the illumination of the Holy Spirit in today.

PRAYER

Lord, I know you love me. I know you care for me. I know you want me to be well. So I thank you. Please help me to see the illumination of the Holy Spirit as I recognize your presence. I am extremely grateful.

MELANIE PADILLA

Day 23

TODAY IS A GOOD DAY

———⁓⁓⁓⊙⊙⊙⊙⁓⁓⁓———

Turn from evil and do good; seek peace and pursue it.
—PSALM 34:14 (KJV)

Today didn't feel like a great day, but it turned out to be one. One spectacular day, I woke up to an intrusive thought. *The sun is about to come up, and you don't like it when that happens.* It was a lie, and I knew it, so instead I thought, *Thank you, Jesus.* I went to the restroom to wash my face and brush my teeth. I turned on a sermon, and the first thing I heard was, "This is the day that the Lord hath made. I will rejoice and be glad in it."

When we get an intrusive thought in the morning, God reminds us of his loving-kindness in all sorts of ways. Choose to wake up with God. Combat those thoughts with the truth of the words of Jesus Christ.

PRAYER

Lord, my God, thank you for this day. I know it is beautiful because you made it. I declare that today is beautiful because you made it. I will be happy today. I will smile. Lord, help me to seek peace and to pursue it.

Day 24

ENJOY AND BE JOYFUL TODAY

*Then I commended enjoyment, because a man has no better thing under the sun
[without God] than to eat and to drink and to be joyful, for that will remain with
him in his toil through the days of his life which God gives him under the sun.*
—ECCLESIASTES 8:15 (AMPC)

"Let's go see a movie or get something to eat." In this case, we did both. I had made plans to go to a theater at 7:00 p.m. to watch a movie with a family member. Because we spent most of our days of the week in the house, we made plans to go and have some enjoyment and time together. We arrived there about two hours early, so gratefully, we were able to go have a few tacos before the movie.

Ecclesiastes 8:5 reminds us that he does not mind when we take a day off to go out to eat and to be joyful. One of the benefits of being a follower of Jesus Christ is that we get to experience him up close and personal. The peace that he leaves with us remains there even while we are experiencing enjoyment with family members and loved ones. He is in our midst there as well, being the intimate Jesus that he is.

PRAYER

Lord Jesus, I thank you for a very beautiful day, as always. I want to seek your peace like the Bible tells me to. Thank you for helping me to seek your peace, to find it, and to hold onto it.

Day 25

SMILE AT SOMEBODY

—⁓∙◦⦿⦿◦∙⁓—

Resist him, standing firm in the faith, because you know that the family of
believers throughout the world is undergoing the same kind of sufferings.
—1 PETER 5:9 (NIV)

Anoint my head, O Lord. My God, let me please not forget that you set me free. I can freely go about my day because your fingerprints are now on display. Psalm 26:12 says, "My feet stand on level ground, in the great congregation I will praise the LORD."

I noticed myself sitting down in church. I knew GOD did not like me to do this, but I somehow found myself doing it anyway. Then I saw this Bible verse later that day about standing up and singing songs in church. I realized that the bible told us to do it as reverence, so I should not even care what other people thought, and I definitely should not hold back because of what the opposition thought.

It just came to my attention today—I recognized this about myself—that all of my prayers are only about *me*. From now on, I am going to write down the issues that I'm going through, whether they are light, medium, or heavy and whether they lasted a second, a minute, or half a day. I am going to write any problem that I experience during the day down and pray for other believers. I am not going to pray selfishly, but instead, I am going to pray for other people who may be at the same moment, going through what I am going through. I will pray for God to help them as he is also helping me. I am not the only one who is going through it. There are other people doing so. I do care about them, and I can empathize with what they are experiencing because I am going through it.

PRAYER

Dear heavenly Father, thank you for your blessings and for all you have done for me. I thank you for all the good plans you have for my life. I pray that you will also bless those around me who may be in need. I also want to pray that you will help me to stand and to give you praise in front of the congregation at church because it is you whom I praise. You are my God. It is my pleasure. Amen.

Day 26

SMARTER FEET

—⁓⧳⧴⧵⁓—

Do not become unequally yoked with unbelievers. For what partnership has righteousness with lawlessness? Or what fellowship has light with darkness?
—2 CORINTHIANS 6:14 (NIV)

JESUS

I noticed that sometimes when I am going up the ladder of success that I can only do it with the help of the Lord my God. Old friends come around and persistently want to chat with me. I ask God, *Why do they keep coming to look for me, Lord? Why do you keep letting this happen?*

It is important to always refer back to the Holy Bible as a *powerful* reference and to answer to all our questions. In Corinthians 6:14, we are reminded as children of the most high God that he does not want us to become syncretized with conversations of worldly people, those who do not follow God, and especially those who have seen his glory but who have stubbornly chosen to deny his will. It says in verse 17 that we are to remain separate from them so that we will continue to be welcomed by God. I will pray for them on my own time because I still have hope, and I know that Jesus can help them just like he is helping me.

But we should choose to follow the Bible's instructions, to guard our hearts, and to carefully watch where the path is going. Proverbs 4:26 says, "Ponder the path of thy feet, and let all thy ways be established."

PRAYER

Jesus, thank you. Lord, please help me to be kind to those around me but also to remember what your words say, to regard them in my life, and to hold tightly to them. I want your words, thoughts, and truth to influence my actions. Thank you.

MELANIE PADILLA

Day 27

ARISE TO GRATITUDE

———∿∾◦⊂∾⊃◦⊙◦⊂∾⊃◦∾∿———

Don't fret or worry. Instead of worrying, pray. Let petitions and praises shape your
worries into prayers, letting God know your concerns. Before you know it, a sense of
God's wholeness, everything coming together for good, will come and settle you down.
It's wonderful what happens when Christ displaces worry at the center of your life.
—PHILIPPIANS 4:6–7 (MSG)

I tried to swat a fly with a composition journal but missed. That is when I first became angry. It was early Tuesday morning. For some reason, I was not looking forward to the day. I got ready to go to the gym, but I did not end up going. I went to Denny's to eat breakfast instead. I spent about an hour there reading the Bible and drinking coffee. I then was late for school because I was not paying attention to the bus that passed right in front of me. I had a lot on my mind. I was actively trying hard to replace each negative thought with a positive one, but I hadn't had much practice doing this, so it was difficult.

As I am reading what I am journaling here, I can point out the issue from the very beginning, which was not necessarily the fly thing. It was the part that I skipped, which I should have done first, before trying to kill the fly. I should have given thanks to God when I woke up the morning. I should have combatted that intrusive thought with the truth I know about Jesus and started my day off with gratitude despite how I was feeling or the thoughts that were in my head trying to consume me.

So despite the way that you wake up and your emotions, feelings, or thoughts, before you get out of bed, say, "Thank you, Jesus, for this beautiful day you have given me." Tell him to help you and that you know it is going to be a good day because he is right there with you at that very moment and throughout the day.

I reached to get my mail, and I got some good news that I was not expecting. I proceeded to thank God. But do not wait until the end of the day or until something good happens to you to give him thanks. God is great—always. Even when I do not believe, it does not mean that God stops working.

PRAYER

Abba, thank you. I praise you. I confide in you. I lay any thoughts that are causing me worry down right here at your feet and trust you to take care of them. I am free.

Day 28

HOPE FOR TODAY

---

*Refuse to worry about tomorrow, but deal with each challenge that comes
your way, one day at a time. Tomorrow will take care of itself.*
—MATTHEW 6:34 (TPT)

It's one day at a time, literally. I have to remind myself of this frequently. There were times when I had multiple, important, and upcoming events, but the Bible said that each day had enough trouble of its own. When I actually practiced the words that the Bible told me and apply them to my everyday life and current struggles, it really did help.

You can reap the benefits of following God's Word by applying it to your current situation. Just try it. Bring your focus back to Jesus and keep practicing that. Relax, breathe, and pray. Do not stress about the troubles of tomorrow. Instead, pray and be at peace.

PRAYER

My Father in heaven, I am your child, and I have the privilege to call you Dad. The Bible says that each day has enough trouble of its own, so please help me to bring my focus back to what the Bible says. I want you to remind me of this scripture about not stressing over tomorrow. I rest in your peace, in Jesus's mighty name. Amen.

MELANIE PADILLA

Day 29

JESUS IS MY BODYGUARD

He has made everything beautiful in its time. He has also set eternity in the human heart; yet [no one can fathom what God has done from beginning to end.
—ECCLESIASTES 3:11 (NIV)

I agree that God has definitely made everything beautiful in its time. Our day may be bombarded with a lot of things, but we must be still and bring our focus back to God every time that we can. Enjoy the day. Notice the small things to be happy about like a cute little baby, a puppy, nature, the birds, etc. I think it is important and very helpful to journal the positive attributes and simple things that you are looking forward to in the day.

I want to give you an example. Imagine a famous person coming out of court. He or she has bodyguards, right? And there are cameras going off and people trying to bombard that person, but the bodyguard's job is to protect him or her. The bodyguard moves the crowd away so that individual can get by safely. I felt like that today. I mean, there was so much negativity going on around me, but God helped me get by. The smiling, little babies and cute puppies—I chose to see the beauty in the day.

Sometimes, negativity surrounds us, and there is nothing we can do about it. It may be a court case you have to attend or forgetting your fully loaded backpack on the train. Jesus loves you, and when unexpected or expected circumstances occur like these, Ecclesiastes 3:11 says to cast *all* your cares on him because he truly cares.

PRAYER

Thank you, Father God. Bless my soul and those around me. I know you love and want me to be healthy, happy, and without stress and worry. Lord, whatever I am dealing with, again, I leave it at your feet right now. Stress, be gone now. I pray this in Jesus's name.

Day 30

JOY, JOY, JOY

———⁓⁓∽◦❍⌒◗◐⌒◦∾⁓⁓———

However, it is written what no eye has seen, what no ear has heard, and what no human mind has conceived, the things God has prepared for those who love him.
—1 CORINTHIANS 2:9 (NIV)

"Everyone, the systems are down and will not be working for a while." I had traveled a long way in hopes of getting a replacement identification card, but it wasn't going to happen the day that I had planned it to. I wondered if I had only prayed for traveling mercies and companionship or consulted with the Lord before I made these plans, it would have been all right. Well, it was a good thing that I was reminded that despite the situation, I knew that Jesus had my back.

I admit that I need his help to remain content and hopefully, at all times. Kings James Version : Philippians 4:11 says, "Not that I speak in respect of want: for I have learned, in whatsoever state I am, therewith to be content." I particularly want to mention that *it is* possible to keep the joy of the Lord within you despite any circumstance and what is going on around you. Be persistent *in not giving up.* Have hope and remain in the peace and joy of God. That is a gift to us because we are children of God.

Did you ever notice a time when you asked God to take care of a particular thing that was bothering you, and later on that day, you were worrying about it again? What do you think that is? I think it is important to react in faith and to remind ourselves that we have already placed that issue in the hands of the most high God so that we no longer have to stress about it. And go about our day. Regarding prayer requests that we have, God answer them, and the Holy Bible tells us that he has much more in store for us that our human mind can conceive. I do not know about you, but I am in awe at trying to understand that part and taking grip of it. Jesus loves you very much.

PRAYER

Thank you, Jesus. I already left that in your hands, and I trust you to take care of it.

MELANIE PADILLA

Day 31

SMILE AT THE SUN

He will appear as your righteousness, as sure as the dawning of a new day.
He will manifest as your justice, as sure and strong as the noonday sun.
Quiet your heart in his presence and wait patiently for YAHWEH.
—PSALMS 37:6–7 (TPT)

I watched the rising of the sun this morning. I witnessed it step-by-step. First, it was dark outside. I slowly started to see an orange, little circle popping up from the clouds. Second, that little circle was the sun, and it started to rise higher and higher like it was being pulled from way up high. Third, once it got very high, it became brighter and brighter. As it got brighter, it produced a white light, which illuminated and provided light to the whole place under it.

The scripture above is telling us to remain calm while he manifests as justice on our side, just as strong as the sun. I encourage you to open your Bible to these verses in any translation and to watch the sun rise and get brighter and brighter.

PRAYER

Thank you, Father God, for all things. You made everything in the whole world. Help me to have the joy of each new dawning day.

LAST PRAYER

Father God, Jehovah, Yahweh, Adonai, Alpha and Omega, my Lord, thank you for sending your Son to save us. Thank you for the precious blood of the Lamb, Jesus. I ask that you forgive all my known and unknown sins. I receive your forgiveness and love. I pray that you bless and anoint this book and that whoever reads it will be blessed. As a special request for all readers, I pray that you pour your love into them so that they may experience your unfailing love and receive forgiveness. May they greatly appreciate realizing and experiencing the meaning of why Jesus died for them on the cross. Father, may they be so grateful that in return, they choose to live for you and seek more of you. In the name of Jesus Christ, amen.